W9-AZM-538

Design Thinking

CHERRY LAKE PUBLISHING • ANN ARBOR, MICHIGAN

by Kristin Fontichiaro

A Note to Adults: Please review the instructions for the activities in this book before allowing children to do them. Be sure to help them with any activities you do not think they can safely complete on their own.

A Note to Kids: Be sure to ask an adult for help with these activities when you need it. Always put your safety first!

Published in the United States of America by Cherry Lake Publishing
Ann Arbor, Michigan
www.cherrylakepublishing.com

Series editor: Kristin Fontichiaro

Library of Congress Cataloging-in-Publication Data
Fontichiaro, Kristin.
    Design thinking / by Kristin Fontichiaro.
        pages cm. — (Makers as innovators)
    Audience: Grade 4 to 6.
    Includes bibliographical references and index.
    ISBN 978-1-63188-870-0 (lib. bdg.) — ISBN 978-1-63188-894-6 (pdf) — ISBN 978-1-63188-882-3 (pbk.) — ISBN 978-1-63188-906-6 (e-book)
    1. Engineering design—Juvenile literature. I. Title.
    TA174.F64 2015
    620'.0042—dc23   2014026640

Cherry Lake Publishing would like to acknowledge the work of The Partnership for 21st Century Skills. Please visit www.p21.org for more information.

Printed in the United States of America
Corporate Graphics Inc.
January 2015

3 1907 00355 5439

Contents

Chapter 1

What Is Design Thinking?

When you think about inventors, what comes to mind? Someone in a rumpled white lab coat working alone behind closed doors, eventually emerging with a miraculous new invention? Some people can create that way. However, many of us could use a little bit of help. Otherwise, we might spend too much time working on inventions that don't do what we need them to do. If we want to create a good invention, we need to make sure it is something people can use.

That's why design thinking is helpful. It's *thinking* about design or maybe even thinking *before* design. It's a process of watching people work, learning how they live their lives, and finding solutions to the difficulties they face each day. Then you gather up all that information, sort it, and look for patterns. Using those patterns, you decide on a plan of action, brainstorm design ideas, make a model or **prototype**, and then

At the grocery store, watch how people use carts. Do kids look comfortable in the seats? Do the wheels turn easily? Is the cart too big? Too small? Design thinkers are curious to know how to make everyday items better.

rework and tweak your invention until it does what it is supposed to.

Lots of people can use design thinking in their jobs. You might use it to create a new product as part of a class project. The IDEO design firm in California is credited with being the first to practice design thinking. They use it to brainstorm ways to make good inventions better, like a **biodegradable** toothbrush or a shopping cart that is lighter and easier to push. Students at the Hasso Plattner Institute of Design at Stanford University, nicknamed the d.school, use design thinking to plan their creations. **Makers** might use it to determine what kind of 3D-printed device works best, how to wire up an Arduino, or what the shape of a stuffed animal should be.

You can use design thinking to design an object, such as a more huggable soft toy for your baby sister. But you can also use design thinking to plan **workflows**. For example, you might help your principal come up with a more efficient way to line kids up as they wait for the bus at the end of the day. You might also use design thinking if you are designing something digital, such as a brochure, an app, or a Web page.

Different Approaches

There are many other names for design thinking. IDEO sometimes calls it human-centered design, because of its strong emphasis on meeting human needs. Some software designers call it contextual inquiry. Everybody practices design thinking a little differently, but the important processes and stages are usually similar. They all provide a set of guidelines for how to tap into the needs, challenges, and ideas of people in order to make something better.

In this book, you'll learn how to use design thinking. Imagine that your classmate Megan travels in a motorized wheelchair. She can get around pretty well by herself, but the buttons in the elevator are too high for her to reach. So whenever she goes to the second floor of your school, a classmate has to go with her. Megan has told you that she feels embarrassed to ask for help. We'll work on Megan's challenge throughout the chapters.

At Stanford University's d.school, ideas are everywhere. Whiteboard walls that move, places to collect brainstorming on sticky notes, and space to spread out all help students and their teachers think big about big problems.

Your first step is to find out more about Megan's challenges in the elevator. It's easy to say, "I know what the problem is, and I know how to fix it." But design thinking asks you to hold off on your hunches and look for **data**. Gathering data can help you see the whole picture. Part of design thinking is the idea that we don't just listen to our own instincts.

The truth is, we don't know for sure what would help Megan. For one thing, we need to ask her for more details. We haven't seen how the height of the elevator buttons compares to the height of her wheel-chair. We don't know if there are other challenges that no one has noticed yet.

So before we can design a solution, we need to get some data. *Data* sounds like an unfriendly word, but it's just a fancy term for numbers and information, so don't be intimidated. It's actually a lot of fun to collect data and figure out what it is telling you.

Chapter 2

Identifying Challenges and Gathering Data

Data can be numbers such as your spelling test scores, your daily temperature when you have the flu, or the number of votes cast in the student council election. Data made up of numbers is called **quantitative data**. When TV commercials talk about how many dentists recommend a certain brand of gum, they are using quantitative

This special wheelchair was designed to help people travel across bumpy, uneven surfaces more easily.

data to convince you that their gum is healthy. Two common ways to gather quantitative data are counting things (such as when your teacher takes morning attendance) and asking people to vote or fill out a multiple-choice **survey**.

Data can also be made up of words and ideas. When your teacher returns an essay you turned in, there are probably comments in the margins about ways to improve your writing. That's **qualitative data**. You can also get qualitative data by interviewing people, reading things they have written, or gathering descriptive words about an object or process. For some projects, doing research at the library can give you important insights into inventions and ideas that others have already tried.

In design thinking, we focus mostly on qualitative data—the words and actions of the real people who will interact with your inventions. But don't be afraid to count items, ask people to vote on ideas, or gather other quantitative data if it fits your project. All design thinking processes are different!

Let's look at Megan's challenge: wanting to use the elevator without having to ask for help. What possible data collection methods could we use?

Most elevators have features to help people in wheelchairs, but elevator designers cannot plan for all potential obstacles.

Observation

We can learn a lot by simply watching what happens. Watch as people come and go using the elevator. Keep an eye on what Megan does and what her helpers do. Does her wheelchair ride smoothly over the gap between the floor and the elevator, or does it bump? Make notes on a clipboard. Watch and take notes as you observe Megan to see if you can identify any patterns or ideas. This method is considered unobtrusive. This means you aren't getting in the way of the people you are watching.

Photographs

Sometimes photographs can help us find things we didn't know we were looking for. Ask for permission to take photographs of Megan's wheelchair. You can capture pictures of the elevator and its panel of buttons, too. Maybe the photos will reveal a clue you hadn't even thought about. They will also help you remember what the situation looks like when you cannot be there in person.

Noting Our Observations of Megan

Take a look at some things we might observe and record in our notes:

Megan's face turns red when she asks her helper to push the elevator button.

Megan often says, "I am sorry to have to ask you for help."

The chair's front wheels stop Megan from getting close enough to the button.

Megan's arms are not long enough to stretch out to reach the button.

Megan thinks she could reach the buttons if her arms were about 6 inches (15 centimeters) longer.

Interviews

Ask Megan and her helpers if you can interview them. You might ask questions while they show you how they use the elevator. If you can't, then sit down with them somewhere else. Remember to avoid leading questions. These are questions that pressure people to respond in a certain way. For example, leading questions might start with phrases like, "Isn't it true," "Don't you agree," and "Don't you believe."

Leading Question to Avoid	Better Question to Use
Isn't it true that you get embarrassed asking for help?	How do you feel when you need to ask for help?
Don't you agree that turning your wheelchair sideways would solve this problem?	Have you ever tried turning your wheelchair sideways to try to reach the buttons? If so, what happened?
Don't you believe that carrying a broom handle would solve this problem?	What have you used in the past to push buttons when riding the elevator alone? What did you like or dislike about that solution?

Learning to ask the right questions, listen carefully to responses, and take good notes takes practice. There are many useful books to help you plan a good interview. See the back of this book for a recommendation.

Maps

You might draw a sketch showing the elevator and Megan's wheelchair. Label it with measurements like the ones described below.

Measurements

How far away is Megan when she tries to reach the button? If she was holding an object in her hand, how long would it have to be to reach the buttons? If she turned her wheelchair sideways, would that put her close enough to the control panel? You'll know if you collect measurements. A ruler or yardstick is fine for short distances, but a tape measure is better for longer measurements.

Open-Ended Survey Questions

Surveys can include open-ended questions. These are questions that ask someone to answer with a sentence or more. Don't provide sample answers—people should respond in their own words. As always, avoid leading questions! Here are some samples of open-ended questions you might ask Megan's helpers:

What do you think would help Megan navigate the elevator on her own?

What else do you do to help Megan besides push the button?

What one thing would make things easier for you on the elevator?

If you try out one method and it doesn't give you the information you were hoping for, try another method! Once you have your data collection methods selected, check with your parent or teacher for permission to start collecting!

Chapter 3

Making Sense of
Your Data

Affinity walls are a great way to organize the data you collect.

Now you have a lot of data to make sense of. Start with your photos, maps, and measurements. You could print them out and make notes in the margins. Or you might use a computer program to make notes on-screen. You are looking for clues that might give you ideas for how to help Megan. If you are working with a group, consider posting your data on a bulletin board or wall so everyone can see it.

Now you want to sort out what you learned during your interviews and observations. A maker-friendly way to do this is by creating an **affinity wall**. To create your affinity wall, you'll need a big blank wall space, a stack of sticky notes, and some markers. If you don't have a blank wall to use, ask if you can tape blank paper to a wall, a door, or even the front of your refrigerator. Most affinity wall projects will fit in a space that measures about 3 feet by 5 feet (0.9 meters by 1.5 meters).

Imagine that you conducted interviews with Megan and three of her helpers. You probably gathered a few pages of handwritten notes on your clipboard. In order to find patterns in the data, we need to separate each piece of information. Write each new idea on a separate sticky note. It might sound silly to copy over your notes, but it really helps when you can see and think about just one idea at a time. Use big letters and dark markers so each idea shows up from far away.

Put a code on each sticky note to help you remember who said what. We'll use H1 for the first helper, H2 for the second helper, and H3 for the third. We'll label Megan's ideas with an M. Label notes from your observations with an O.

Once you have rewritten your notes onto the sticky notes, put them up on the wall one at a time. Cluster similar ideas near one another. You might sort your

Clustering Data

Here are some examples of clustered interview data and observed data:

Helper Attitudes

H1: Wants to help Megan

H2: Loves missing class!

H3: Likes to help

Problems with Helper System

H1: Doesn't like leaving class

H3: Misses spelling tests to help Megan and has to stay in for recess to make it up

M: Embarrassed to receive help

O: Megan blushes when asking for help—embarrassed?

Problem Is Only a Few Inches Away from Being Solved

H1: Feels silly pushing the button when it is only 2 or 3 inches (5 or 8 cm)
too far away

M: Hopes to grow—is only a few inches away from being able to reach

Possible Places to Store a Solution

H1: Megan hangs her backpack over one of the push handles and can reach it

H2: Hang something from Megan's seat?

M: Keeps keys hanging from armrest

M: Wears fanny pack to store small items

M: Hangs backpack from rear handles

Turning Sideways

H2: Turning wheelchair sideways doesn't work

H2: Grips on wheels stick out too far to turn sideways

H3: Hand grips on wheels stick out too far

H3: Megan can't reach buttons even if turned sideways

M: Doesn't use handrails on wheels on side of wheelchair—uses motorized
controls instead

Great! Those interviews gave us plenty of information to move forward. And sorting the notes into clusters helps us see themes, or big ideas, that are shared between multiple people.

For this project, it would be best to use sticky notes that are all the same color.

sticky notes several times until they seem grouped correctly. Then make a new note to stick at the top of each cluster that states its main idea.

Chapter 4

Brainstorming Solutions

Now that we see some themes emerging, we can start to think of possible solutions. Two helpers pointed out that Megan can't reach the buttons even when she turns her wheelchair sideways. This is

Design thinking helps inventors find new ways to use existing products, too. What do you think the design team learned when designing the backless seat and front wheel of this racing wheelchair?

Objects such as the keys Megan hangs from her chair can provide inspiration for your design solutions.

because there are hula hoop–shaped handrails around each wheel rim that stick out too far. But did you see what Megan said? She said she doesn't use those handrails. Add those facts together, and one solution could be to ask Megan's parents and medical advisers if the handrails could be removed. Maybe that will solve the problem!

Can you see another possibility? There were two notes that said Megan is only a few inches away from being able to reach the buttons. She might outgrow the problem eventually. But maybe giving her an object just a few inches long would let her poke at the buttons herself. She already hangs things from her waist (fanny pack), armrest (key ring), and rear handles (backpack). So the item could hang on one of those places when not needed. Could you invent an object like that?

Multiple Solutions

In this example, we identified two possible solutions: removing the circular handrails from the side of Megan's wheelchair, and creating an object that she can hold and use to push the button. You might pick either one or both of these possibilities to explore. You might end up with two good solutions for Megan. This gives her the power to pick which one she wants. Or you might find that one works better than the other. The fun part of design thinking is exploring the choices!

Chapter 5

Prototyping, Testing, and Revising

I n chapter three, we figured out that we could create an object that could hang from Megan's chair or waist and reach at least 3 inches (8 cm) farther than her fingers can. You might be thinking that this is a great time to run over to the computer, design a 3D

A 3D printer can be a good way to create simple, plastic objects to test design ideas.

model, and use a 3D printer to create a plastic object. But if the object doesn't work, we will have lost hours of valuable time.

Instead, let's make a quick rough draft of something that might work and test it out. Rough drafts of inventions are called prototypes. Though we're working on a physical object that Megan can use, prototypes can also be anything from rough sketches of Web page or app designs to written outlines of possible procedures to improve a bus line. Whatever you're working on, you want to capture ideas quickly so you can test them. Save beauty for later. We're working on functionality now!

Prototypes can be built from almost anything. This includes wood or fabric scraps, LEGO bricks, modeling clay, cardboard, or even items you find in the recycling bin. The goal is to make something quickly and cheaply so people can see your ideas right away. In most cases, you need little to no money to create a prototype. Just use your imagination!

Looking around your classroom, you see a ruler. It's 12 inches (30 cm) long and has holes so you can snap it into a three-ring binder. It also has a metal edge along one side. Instead of building something, you decide to use this ruler as your prototype. You tie a shoelace through one of the holes and help Megan hang it from her wheelchair's armrest. Together, you head for the elevator to try it out. Megan mentions that the ruler is hanging in a perfect place. Great! One part of the problem is solved.

Your job is to observe the prototype in action. Megan's job is to see if she can use it to push the button. It works! But the metal ruler edge scrapes against the elevator panel, leaving a scratch. It isn't comfortable against Megan's hand, either. This gives you important information. Now you know that the ideal product should not have sharp edges. You borrow a pair of pliers from the custodian and pull off the metal edge.

Megan tries again. This time, you realize that the ruler is a bit too wide for the button, so she has to use the ruler's corner to activate it. You also notice that Megan's disability makes her hand shake a bit, so it's hard for her to aim the corner of the ruler right at the center of the elevator button. The length is right,

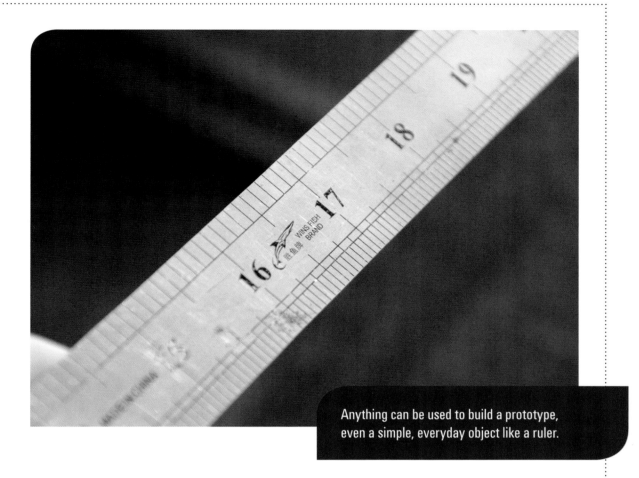

Anything can be used to build a prototype, even a simple, everyday object like a ruler.

though. Now we know that the final product needs the following features:

- A way to be hung from Megan's wheelchair
- A length of about 12 inches (30 cm) so there is room for Megan's hand to grip it and for her to reach the buttons without stretching
- A comfortable grip so Megan can hold on to it securely

Tips for Practicing Design Thinking in a Group

If you are practicing design thinking with a group, be patient and allow people to suggest many solutions before deciding which one to pursue. This will keep the ideas flowing. Ask someone to make a list of the possible solutions.

You might find it helpful to set some guidelines for behavior when you are brainstorming solutions or making decisions about your prototype. When people get excited or frustrated about challenges and solutions, they might interrupt, accidentally hurt someone's feelings by shooting down an idea, or talk over someone else. Another problem is that the group might get off track. Someone might want to talk about solutions when the group is still analyzing the data. Ask someone to be the moderator. A moderator is a person who helps guide the discussion and keep it focused. This can make sure your work is calm and rewarding.

- A blunt end so it feels stable when Megan uses it to press the button
- An end that is smaller than the elevator button

You have used a simple prototype to figure out exactly what Megan needs. You make an appointment with your nearby **makerspace**, where the staff helps you create a perfect device. It has a hole in it

Some types of elevator buttons would be hard to press with an object that is too large.

and a shoelace so it can hang from Megan's armrest. It has golf tape wrapped around one end to improve Megan's grip if her hand shakes. The end is flat, not pointed. It is also just smaller than the elevator buttons. This ensures that Megan can make good contact with the button every time she pushes it.

Congratulations! Through observation, organizing data, prototyping, and keeping an open mind, you've created a perfect solution to help Megan become more independent. What will you work on next?

Glossary

affinity wall (uh-FINN-ih-tee WALL) a place for clustering notes to help you understand the big picture

biodegradable (bye-oh-di-GRAY-duh-buhl) able to be broken down by natural processes

data (DAY-tuh) information collected in a place so that something can be done with it

makers (MAY-kurz) people who use their creativity to make something

makerspace (MAY-kur-spays) a place containing tools and other equipment where makers can share ideas and work on projects

prototype (PROH-tuh-tipe) the first version of an invention that tests an idea to see if it will work

qualitative data (KWAH-lih-tay-tiv DAY-tuh) data made up of words or ideas

quantitative data (KWAN-tih-tay-tiv DAY-tuh) data made up of numbers

survey (SUR-vay) a study of the opinions or experiences of a group of people, based on their responses to questions

themes (THEEMZ) the main subjects or ideas of something

workflows (WERK-flowz) lists of actions to be completed in a certain order

Find Out More

BOOKS

Cook, Eric. *Prototyping*. Ann Arbor, MI: Cherry Lake Publishing, 2015.

Truesdell, Ann. *Fire Away: Asking Great Interview Questions*. Ann Arbor, MI: Cherry Lake Publishing, 2013.

WEB SITES

ABC *Nightline*—IDEO Shopping Cart
http://youtu.be/M66ZU2PCIcM
Watch IDEO team members use design thinking to create a new kind of shopping cart in this clip from ABC's *Nightline*.

IDEO—Human-Centered Design Toolkit
www.ideo.com/work/human-centered-design-toolkit
Learn strategies for using design thinking principles to help others. Ask an adult before creating an account here.

Index

About the Author

Kristin Fontichiaro teaches at the University of Michigan School of Information, where her students learn and practice a form of design thinking.